URBAN HATS
Made with the Knook™

Knooking is the new knitting!

The Knook is a specialized crochet hook that creates true knitted fabric, while the attached cord completely prevents dropped stitches! Use the Knook to make these 7 hats quickly and easily. Clear instructions on the basic technique start on page 27, and are included for both right-hand & left-hand stitching, while photos illustrate each step. You'll also find excellent videos at LeisureArts.com that show every stitch step-by-step. Great for beginners or anyone that would like to learn to knit the easy way—the Knook makes knitting fun!

Get more! Visit LeisureArts.com for additional Knook pattern books, easy instructions, and our clear how-to videos! Look for the Knook at your local retailer or LeisureArts.com!

TABLE OF CONTENTS

LEISURE ARTS, INC.
Little Rock, Arkansas

2-STITCH CABLE PATTERN

■■■□ INTERMEDIATE

Size: Small/Medium {Large/X-Large}
Fits Head Circumference: 19{21}"/48.5{53.5} cm

Size Note: Instructions are written for size Small/
Medium with size Large/X-Large in braces { }.
Instructions will be easier to read if you circle all
the numbers pertaining to your size. If only one
number is given, it applies to both sizes.

MATERIALS
Medium Weight Yarn **MEDIUM 4**
  [3.5 ounces, 210 yards
  (100 grams, 192 meters) per skein]: 1 skein
Knooks, sizes G (4 mm) **and** H (5 mm) **or**
  sizes needed for gauge
Marker
Yarn needle

GAUGE: With larger size Knook, in Body pattern,
        18 sts (2 repeats) and
        24 rows/rnds = 4" (10 cm)

Techniques used:
- P2 tog *(Fig. 17, page 26)*
- Slip 1 as if to **knit**, K1, PSSO *(Figs. 18a & b, page 26)*

Hat is worked with **wrong** side facing throughout.

RIBBING
With smaller size Knook, ch 90{99}.

Foundation Rnd: Bring first ch around to meet
last ch made, making sure that the ch isn't twisted,
and pick up a st in first 89{98} chs *(see Circular Knitting, page 23)*. Place a marker to indicate the
beginning of the rnd: 90{99} sts.

Rnd 1 (Wrong side): ★ K2, P1, K1, P1, K2, P2;
repeat from ★ around.

Repeat Rnd 1 for pattern until Ribbing measures
approximately 1½" (4 cm) from foundation ch
edge.

Rnd 1: (K7, P2) around.

Rnd 2: (K7, C2B) around.

Rnds 3 and 4: (K7, P2) around.

Repeat Rnds 2-4 for pattern until Hat measures approximately 7" (18 cm) from foundation ch edge, ending by working Rnd 2.

SHAPING

Rnd 1: ★ Slip 1, K1, PSSO, K5, P2; repeat from ★ around: 80{88} sts.

Rnd 2: (K6, P2) around.

Rnd 3: ★ Slip 1, K1, PSSO, K4, C2B; repeat from ★ around: 70{77} sts.

Rnd 4: (K5, P2) around.

Rnd 5: ★ Slip 1, K1, PSSO, K3, P2; repeat from ★ around: 60{66} sts.

Rnd 6: (K4, C2B) around.

Rnd 7: ★ Slip 1, K1, PSSO, K2, P2; repeat from ★ around: 50{55} sts.

Rnd 8: (K3, P2) around.

Rnd 9: ★ Slip 1, K1, PSSO, K1, C2B; repeat from ★ around: 40{44} sts.

Rnd 10: (K2, P2) around.

Rnd 11: ★ Slip 1, K1, PSSO, P2; repeat from ★ around: 30{33} sts.

Rnd 12: (K1, C2B) around.

Rnd 13: (K1, P2) around.

Rnd 14: (K1, P2 tog) around: 20{22} sts.

Cut yarn leaving an 8" (20.5 cm) length for sewing. Thread yarn needle with end and slip remaining sts from cord onto needle; remove cord. Pull **tightly** to close and secure end.

BODY

Change to larger size Knook.

To work Cable 2 Back *(abbreviated C2B)*, skip next st, pull skipped st to **back** of work on cord, purl next st *(Fig. 1)*, holding skipped st **behind** last st made, purl skipped st *(Fig. 2)*.

Fig. 1

Fig. 2

4-STITCH CABLE PATTERN

Size: Small/Medium {Large/X-Large}
Fits Head Circumference: 19{21}"/48.5{53.5} cm

Size Note: Instructions are written for size Small/Medium with size Large/X-Large in braces { }. Instructions will be easier to read if you circle all the numbers pertaining to your size. If only one number is given, it applies to both sizes.

MATERIALS

Medium Weight Yarn **④**
  [3.5 ounces, 210 yards
  (100 grams, 192 meters) per skein]: 1 skein
Knooks, sizes G (4 mm) **and** I (5.5 mm) **or**
  sizes needed for gauge
Marker
Yarn needle

GAUGE: With larger size Knook,
    in Stockinette Stitch,
    16 sts and 22 rows/rnds = 4" (10 cm)

Techniques used:
- Increases *(see Increases, pages 24 & 25)*
- K2 tog *(Figs. 16a & b, page 25)*
- Slip 1 as if to **knit**, K1, PSSO *(Figs. 18a & b, page 26)*
- K3 tog *(Figs. 19a & b, page 26)*

Hat is worked with **wrong** side facing throughout.

RIBBING

With smaller size Knook, ch 84{92}.

Foundation Rnd: Bring first ch around to meet last ch made, making sure that the ch isn't twisted, and pick up a st in first 83{91} chs *(see Circular Knitting, page 23)*. Place a marker to indicate the beginning of the rnd: 84{92} sts.

Rnd 1 (Wrong side)**:** (K2, P2) around.

Repeat Rnd 1 for pattern until Ribbing measures approximately 1¹/₂" (4 cm) from foundation ch edge, increasing 12{8} sts evenly spaced across last rnd *(see Increasing Evenly Across a Row or Rnd, page 24)*: 96{100} sts.

BODY

Change to larger size Knook.

To work **Cable 4 Back** *(abbreviated C4B)*, skip next 2 sts, pull skipped sts to **back** of work on cord, purl next 2 sts *(Fig. 3)*, holding skipped sts **behind** last 2 sts made, purl 2 skipped sts *(Fig. 4)*, purling them in order.

Fig. 3

Fig. 4

Rnds 1 and 2: ★ K 20{21}, P4; repeat from ★ around.

Rnd 3: ★ K 20{21}, C4B; repeat from ★ around.

Rnds 4-7: ★ K 20{21}, P4; repeat from ★ around.

Repeat Rnds 3-7 for pattern until Hat measures approximately 7" (18 cm) from foundation ch edge, ending by working Rnd 3.

SHAPING

Rnd 1: ★ (Slip 1, K1, PSSO) twice, K 16{17}, P4; repeat from ★ around: 88{92} sts.

Rnd 2: ★ K 18{19}, P4; repeat from ★ around.

Rnd 3: ★ (Slip 1, K1, PSSO) twice, K 14{15}, P4; repeat from ★ around: 80{84} sts.

Rnd 4: ★ K 16{17}, P4; repeat from ★ around.

Rnd 5: ★ (Slip 1, K1, PSSO) twice, K 12{13}, C4B; repeat from ★ around: 72{76} sts.

Rnd 6: ★ K 14{15}, P4; repeat from ★ around.

Rnd 7: ★ (Slip 1, K1, PSSO) twice, K 10{11}, P4; repeat from ★ around: 64{68} sts.

Rnd 8: ★ K 12{13}, P4; repeat from ★ around.

Rnd 9: ★ (Slip 1, K1, PSSO) twice, K8{9}, P4; repeat from ★ around: 56{60} sts.

Rnd 10: ★ K 10{11}, C4B; repeat from ★ around.

Rnd 11: ★ (Slip 1, K1, PSSO) twice, K6{7}, P4; repeat from ★ around: 48{52} sts.

Rnd 12: ★ K8{9}, P4; repeat from ★ around.

Rnd 13: ★ (Slip 1, K1, PSSO) twice, K4{5}, P4; repeat from ★ around: 40{44} sts.

Rnd 14: ★ K6{7}, P4; repeat from ★ around.

Rnd 15: ★ (Slip 1, K1, PSSO) twice, K2{3}, C4B; repeat from ★ around: 32{36} sts.

Rnd 16: ★ K4{5}, P4; repeat from ★ around.

Rnd 17: ★ (Slip 1, K1, PSSO) twice, K 0{1} *(see Zeros, page 23)*, P4; repeat from ★ around: 24{28} sts.

Rnd 18: ★ K2{3}, P4; repeat from ★ around.

Rnd 19: ★ K2{3} tog, P4; repeat from ★ around: 20 sts.

Cut yarn leaving an 8" (20.5 cm) length for sewing. Thread yarn needle with end and slip remaining sts from cord onto needle; remove cord. Pull **tightly** to close and secure end.

CHEVRON LACE PATTERN

◐◼◻◻ **EASY +**

Size: Small/Medium {Large/X-Large}
Fits Head Circumference: 19{21}"/48.5{53.5} cm

Size Note: Instructions are written for size Small/Medium with size Large/X-Large in braces { }. Instructions will be easier to read if you circle all the numbers pertaining to your size. If only one number is given, it applies to both sizes.

MATERIALS
Medium Weight Yarn **[MEDIUM 4]**
 [6 ounces, 315 yards
 (170 grams, 288 meters) per skein]: 1 skein
Knooks, sizes G (4 mm) **and** H (5 mm) {I (5.5 mm)}
 or sizes needed for gauge
Marker
Yarn needle

GAUGE: With larger size Knook,
 in Stockinette Stitch, 18{16} sts
 and 24{22} rows = 4" (10 cm)

Techniques used:
- YO *(Fig. 15, page 25)*
- K2 tog *(Figs. 16a & b, page 25)*
- P2 tog *(Fig. 17, page 26)*
- Slip 1 as if to **knit**, K1, PSSO *(Figs. 18a & b, page 26)*

RIBBING
With smaller size Knook, ch 90{94}.

Foundation Rnd: Bring first ch around to meet last ch made, making sure that the ch isn't twisted, and pick up a st in first 89{93} chs *(see Circular Knitting, page 23)*. Place a marker to indicate the beginning of the rnd: 90{94} sts.

Rnd 1 (Right side)**:** (K1, P1) around.

Repeat Rnd 1 for pattern until Ribbing measures approximately 2" (5 cm) from foundation ch edge.

BODY
Change to larger size Knook.

Small/Medium Size ONLY - Rnd 1: Purl around.

Large/X-Large Size ONLY - Rnd 1: (P 22, P2 tog, P 21, P2 tog) twice: 90 sts.

BOTH Sizes - Rnd 2: Purl around.

Rnd 3: Knit around.

Rnd 4: ★ YO, K2, K2 tog, slip 1, K1, PSSO, K2, YO, K1; repeat from ★ around.

On the round following a YO, you must be careful to treat it as a stitch by knitting it as instructed.

Rnd 5: Knit around.

Rnds 6-9: Repeat Rnds 4 and 5 twice.

Rnds 10 and 11: Purl around.

Rnds 12-30: Repeat Rnds 3-11 twice, then repeat Rnd 3 once **more**.

SHAPING
Rnd 1: (Slip 1, K1, PSSO, K7) around: 80 sts.

Rnd 2 AND ALL EVEN NUMBERED RNDS: Knit around.

Rnd 3: (Slip 1, K1, PSSO, K6) around: 70 sts.

Rnd 5: (Slip 1, K1, PSSO, K5) around: 60 sts.

Rnd 7: (Slip 1, K1, PSSO, K4) around: 50 sts.

Rnd 9: (Slip 1, K1, PSSO, K3) around: 40 sts.

Rnd 11: (Slip 1, K1, PSSO, K2) around: 30 sts.

Rnd 13: (Slip 1, K1, PSSO, K1) around: 20 sts.

Rnd 15: (Slip 1, K1, PSSO) around: 10 sts.

Cut yarn leaving an 8" (20.5 cm) length for sewing. Thread yarn needle with end and slip remaining sts from cord onto needle; remove cord.
Pull **tightly** to close and secure end.

CIRCLES HAT

Size: Small/Medium {Large/X-Large}
Fits Head Circumference: 19{21}"/48.5{53.5} cm

Size Note: Instructions are written for size Small/ Medium with size Large/X-Large in braces { }. Instructions will be easier to read if you circle all the numbers pertaining to your size. If only one number is given, it applies to both sizes.

MATERIALS

Medium Weight Yarn
    [3.5 ounces, 200 yards
    (100 grams, 182 meters) per skein]: 1 skein
Knooks, sizes G (4 mm) **and** H (5 mm) **or** sizes
    needed for gauge
Marker
1" (26 mm) Button
Yarn needle

GAUGE: With larger size Knook,
            in Stockinette Stitch,
            18 sts and 24 rows = 4" (10 cm)
            With smaller size Knook,
            in Garter Stitch,
            16 sts and 34 rows = 4" (10 cm)

Techniques used:
- Increases *(see Increases, pages 24 & 25)*
- K2 tog *(Figs. 16a & b, page 25)*

BAND

With smaller size Knook and leaving an 8" (20.5 cm) length for sewing, ch 87{95}.

Foundation Row: Pick up 81{89} sts on foundation ch, leaving last 5 chs unworked for button loop: 82{90} sts.

Rows 1-11: Knit across.

Row 12: Bind off 6 sts in **knit** for flap, knit across increasing 4 sts evenly spaced *(see Increasing Evenly Across A Row or Rnd, page 24)*: 80{88} sts.

BODY

Change to larger size Knook.

Increase Row (Right side)**:** (K7, knit increase in next st) around; do **not** turn, place a marker to indicate the beginning of the next rnd *(Fig. 10, page 23)*: 90{99} sts.

Being careful not to twist Band, bring end of Band around, overlapping the end with the flap, and begin Rnd 1 working in the first st of end.

Rnd 1: (K8, P1) around.

Rnd 2: K7, P1, (K8, P1) around to last st, K1.

Rnd 3: K6, P1, (K8, P1) around to last 2 sts, K2.

Rnd 4: K5, P1, (K8, P1) around to last 3 sts, K3.

Rnd 5: K4, P1, (K8, P1) around to last 4 sts, K4.

Rnd 6: K3, P1, (K8, P1) around to last 5 sts, K5.

Rnd 7: K2, P1, (K8, P1) around to last 6 sts, K6.

Rnd 8: K1, P1, (K8, P1) around to last 7 sts, K7.

Rnd 9: (P1, K8) around.

Rnds 10-36: Repeat Rnds 1-9, 3 times.

SHAPING

Rnd 1: (K6, K2 tog, P1) around: 80{88} sts.

Rnd 2: K6, P1, (K7, P1) around to last st, K1.

Rnd 3: K3, K2 tog, P1, (K5, K2 tog, P1) around to last 2 sts, K2: 70{77} sts.

Rnd 4: K3, P1, (K6, P1) around to last 3 sts, K3.

Rnd 5: (K2 tog, P1, K4) around: 60{66} sts.

Rnd 6: (P1, K5) around.

Rnd 7: (K3, K2 tog, P1) around: 50{55} sts.

Rnd 8: K3, P1, (K4, P1) around to last st, K1.

Rnd 9: (K2 tog, P1, K2) around: 40{44} sts.

Rnd 10: (P1, K3) around.

Rnd 11: (K1, K2 tog, P1) around: 30{33} sts.

Rnd 12: K1, P1, (K2, P1) around to last st, K1.

Rnd 13: (P1, K2 tog) around: 20{22} sts.

Rnd 14: (K1, P1) around.

Cut yarn leaving an 8" (20.5 cm) length for sewing. Thread yarn needle with end and slip remaining sts from cord onto needle; remove cord.
Pull **tightly** to close and secure end.

Thread yarn needle with beginning end and secure end at top corner of flap to form button loop.
Sew button to Band opposite button loop.

EASY LACE PATTERN

Size: Small/Medium {Large/X-Large}
Fits Head Circumference: 19{21}"/48.5{53.5} cm

Size Note: Instructions are written for size Small/
Medium with size Large/X-Large in braces { }.
Instructions will be easier to read if you circle all
the numbers pertaining to your size. If only one
number is given, it applies to both sizes.

MATERIALS

Medium Weight Yarn 🄬
[3.5 ounces, 177 yards
(100 grams, 162 meters) per skein]: 1 skein
Knooks, sizes G (4 mm) **and** H (5 mm) {I (5.5 mm)}
or sizes needed for gauge
Marker
Yarn needle

GAUGE: With larger size Knook, in Body pattern,
18 sts (2 repeats slightly stretched)
and 22 rows = 4{4¹/₄}"/10{10.75} cm

Techniques used:
• Increases *(see Increases, pages 24 & 25)*
• YO *(Fig. 15, page 25)*
• K2 tog *(Figs. 16a & b, page 25)*
• P2 tog *(Fig. 17, page 26)*
• Slip 1 as if to **knit**, K1, PSSO *(Figs. 18a & b, page 26)*

RIBBING

With smaller size Knook, ch 90{99}.

Foundation Rnd: Bring first ch around to meet
last ch made, making sure that the ch isn't twisted,
and pick up a st in first 89{98} chs *(see Circular
Knitting, page 23)*. Place a marker to indicate the
beginning of the rnd: 90{99} sts.

Rnd 1 (Right side)**:** (K2, P1) around.

Repeat Rnd 1 for pattern until Ribbing measures
approximately 2" (5 cm) from foundation ch edge
increasing 9{0} sts evenly spaced on last rnd *(see
Zeros, page 23, and Increasing Evenly Across A
Row or Rnd, page 24)*: 99 sts.

BODY

Change to larger size Knook.

Rnd 1: (K8, P1) around.

Rnd 2: ★ K3, slip 1, K1, PSSO, YO, K3, P1; repeat
from ★ around.

On the round following a YO, you must be careful
to treat it as a stitch by knitting it as instructed.

Rnd 3: (K8, P1) around.

Rnd 4: ★ K3, YO, K2 tog, K3, P1; repeat from ★
around.

Repeat Rnds 1-4 for pattern until Hat measures approximately 6½" (16.5 cm) from foundation ch edge, ending by working Rnd 4.

SHAPING

Rnd 1: (K6, K2 tog, P1) around: 88 sts.

Rnd 2: ★ K3, slip 1, K1, PSSO, YO, K2, P1; repeat from ★ around.

Rnd 3: ★ Slip 1, K1, PSSO, K5, P1; repeat from ★ around: 77 sts.

Rnd 4: ★ K2, YO, K2 tog, K2, P1; repeat from ★ around.

Rnd 5: (K4, K2 tog, P1) around: 66 sts.

Rnd 6: ★ K2, slip 1, K1, PSSO, YO, K1, P1; repeat from ★ around.

Rnd 7: ★ Slip 1, K1, PSSO, K3, P1; repeat from ★ around: 55 sts.

Rnd 8: ★ K1, YO, K2 tog, K1, P1; repeat from ★ around.

Rnd 9: (K4, P1) around.

Rnd 10: ★ K1, slip 1, K1, PSSO, YO, K1, P1; repeat from ★ around.

Rnd 11: ★ K1, slip 1, K1, PSSO, K1, P1; repeat from ★ around: 44 sts.

Rnd 12: ★ K1, YO, K2 tog, P1; repeat from ★ around.

Rnd 13: (K2, P2 tog) around: 33 sts.

Rnd 14: (K2, P1) around.

Rnd 15: (K2 tog, P1) around: 22 sts.

Rnd 16: (K1, P1) around.

Cut yarn leaving an 8" (20.5 cm) length for sewing. Thread yarn needle with end and slip remaining sts from cord onto needle; remove cord. Pull **tightly** to close and secure end.

SIDEWAYS GARTER STITCH HAT

Shown on page 19.

◖◼◻◻ **EASY +**

Size: Small/Medium {Large/X-Large}
Fits Head Circumference: 19{21}"/48.5{53.5} cm

Size Note: Instructions are written for size Small/Medium with size Large/X-Large in braces { }. Instructions will be easier to read if you circle all the numbers pertaining to your size. If only one number is given, it applies to both sizes.

MATERIALS

Medium Weight Yarn 🧶 **4**
[3.5 ounces, 170 yards
(100 grams, 156 meters) per skein]:
Magenta **and** Grey - 1 skein **each** color
Knook, size I (5.5 mm) **or** size needed for gauge
Marker
Stitch holder
Yarn needle

GAUGE: In Garter Stitch,
15 sts and 30 rows = 4" (10 cm)

Hat is worked from side-to-side.

BODY

With Grey, ch 37.

Foundation Row: Pick up 36 sts on foundation ch: 37 sts.

Row 1 (Right side): (K1, P1) 3 times, K 30, slip last st onto st holder inserting st holder from **left** to **right (now and throughout)** *(Fig. 5)*: 36 sts (one st on st holder).

Fig. 5

Row 2: Knit across to last 7 sts, P1, (K1, P1) 3 times.

Row 3: (K1, P1) 3 times, K 28, slip next 2 sts onto same st holder; **turn**: 34 sts (3 sts on st holder).

Row 4: Knit across to last 7 sts, P1, (K1, P1) 3 times.

Row 10: Knit across to last 7 sts, P1, (K1, P1) 3 times.

Row 11: (K1, P1) 3 times, K 22, slip next 2 sts onto same st holder; **turn:** 28 sts (9 sts on st holder).

Row 12: Knit across to last 7 sts, P1, (K1, P1) 3 times.

Row 13: (K1, P1) 3 times, K 21, slip next st onto same st holder; **turn:** 27 sts (10 sts on st holder).

Row 14: Knit across to last 7 sts, P1, (K1, P1) 3 times.

Row 15: (K1, P1) 3 times, K 21, knit first 4 sts on st holder, drop Magenta; with Grey *(Fig. 11, page 24)*, knit last 6 sts on st holder: 37 sts.

Row 16: K6, cut Grey; with Magenta, knit across to last 7 sts, P1, (K1, P1) 3 times, cut Magenta.

Row 17: With Grey, (K1, P1) 3 times, K 30, slip last st onto st holder: 36 sts (one st on st holder).

Rows 18 thru 126{142}: Repeat Rows 2-17, 6{7} times; then repeat Rows 2-14 once **more**.

Including sts from st holder, bind off all sts **loosely** in **knit**, leaving a long end for sewing.

Thread yarn needle with long end and sew last row and foundation ch edge together for back seam.

Row 5: (K1, P1) 3 times, K 27, slip next st onto same st holder; **turn:** 33 sts (4 sts on st holder).

Row 6: Knit across to last 7 sts, P1, (K1, P1) 3 times.

Row 7: (K1, P1) 3 times, K 25, slip next 2 sts onto same st holder; **turn:** 31 sts (6 sts on st holder).

Row 8: Knit across to last 7 sts, P1, (K1, P1) 3 times.

Row 9: With Magenta, (K1, P1) 3 times, K 24, slip next st onto same st holder; **turn:** 30 sts (7 sts on st holder).

TASSEL HAT

Size: Small/Medium {Large/X-Large}
Fits Head Circumference: 19{21}"/48.5{53.5} cm

Size Note: Instructions are written for size Small/Medium with size Large/X-Large in braces { }. Instructions will be easier to read if you circle all the numbers pertaining to your size. If only one number is given, it applies to both sizes.

MATERIALS

Medium Weight Yarn (4)
  [4 ounces, 204 yards
  (113 grams, 187 meters) per skein]: 1 skein
Knook, size H (5 mm) **or** size needed for gauge
Yarn needle

GAUGE: In Garter Stitch,
        17 sts and 34 rows = 4" (10 cm)

BODY

Ch 42{46}.

Foundation Row: Pick up 41{45} sts on foundation ch: 42{46} sts.

Row 1: Knit across.

Repeat Row 1 for pattern until Body measures approximately 15{17}"/38{43} cm from foundation ch edge.

Bind off all sts **loosely** in **knit.**

FINISHING

Thread yarn needle with a 16" (40.5 cm) length of yarn. Fold Body in half, matching bound off edge to foundation ch edge, and sew each side seam.

TASSEL

Make 2 tassels as follows:

Cut a piece of cardboard 3¹/₂" (9 cm) square. Wind yarn around cardboard approximately 30 times. Cut an 18" (45.5 cm) length of yarn and insert it under all of the strands at the top of the cardboard; pull up **tightly** and tie securely. Leave the yarn ends long enough to attach the tassel. Cut the yarn at the opposite end of the cardboard and then remove it *(Fig. 6)*. Cut a 6" (15 cm) length of yarn and wrap it **tightly** around the tassel twice, ³/₄" (2 cm) below the top *(Fig. 7)*; tie securely. Trim the ends. Sew tassels to top of each point of Hat.

Fig. 6

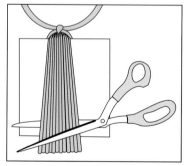

Fig. 7

GENERAL INSTRUCTIONS

ABBREVIATIONS

C2B	Cable 2 Back
C4B	Cable 4 Back
ch(s)	chain(s)
cm	centimeters
K	knit
M1	Make One
M1P	Make One Purl
mm	millimeters
P	purl
PSSO	pass slipped stitch over
Rnd(s)	Round(s)
st(s)	stitch(es)
tog	together
YO	yarn over

★ — work instructions following ★ as many **more** times as indicated in addition to the first time.

( ) or [ ] — work enclosed instructions **as many** times as specified by the number immediately following **or** contains explanatory remarks.

colon (:) — the number(s) given after a colon at the end of a row or round denotes the number of stitches you should have on that row or round.

front vs. **back** side — As you are working, the side facing you is the **front** of your work; the **back** is the side away from you.

right side vs. **wrong** side — on the finished piece, the right side of your work is the side the public will see.

GAUGE

Gauge is the number of stitches and rows in every inch of your knit piece. Exact gauge is essential for proper size. Before beginning your project, make a sample swatch using the yarn and Knook specified in the individual instructions. After completing the swatch, measure it, counting your stitches and rows or rounds carefully. If your swatch is larger or smaller than specified, make another, changing Knook size to get the correct gauge. Keep trying until you find the size Knook that will give you the specified gauge.

KNOOK TERMINOLOGY	
UNITED STATES	**INTERNATIONAL**
gauge =	tension
bind off =	cast off
yarn over (YO) =	yarn forward (yfwd) **or** yarn around needle (yrn)

Yarn Weight Symbol & Names	SUPER FINE 1	FINE 2	LIGHT 3	MEDIUM 4	BULKY 5	SUPER BULKY 6
Type of Yarns in Category	Sock, Fingering Baby	Sport, Baby	DK, Light Worsted	Worsted, Afghan, Aran	Chunky, Craft, Rug	Bulky, Roving
Knook Gauge Ranges in Stockinette St to 4" (10 cm)	27-32 sts	23-26 sts	21-24 sts	16-20 sts	12-15 sts	6-11 sts
Advised Knook Size Range	B-1 to D-3	D-3 to F-5	F-5 to G-6	G-6 to I-9	I-9 to K-10½	M-13 and larger

■□□□ **BEGINNER**	Projects for first-time stitchers using basic knit and purl stitches. Minimal shaping.
■■□□ **EASY**	Projects using basic stitches, repetitive stitch patterns, simple color changes, knitting in the round techniques, and simple shaping and finishing.
■■■□ **INTERMEDIATE**	Projects with a variety of stitches, such as basic cables and lace, simple intarsia, and mid-level shaping and finishing.
■■■■ **EXPERIENCED**	Projects using advanced techniques and stitches, such as short rows, fair isle, more intricate intarsia, cables, lace patterns, and numerous color changes.

CIRCULAR KNITTING

Chain the required number of stitches. Bring the first chain around to meet the last chain made, making sure that the chain isn't twisted (*Fig. 8*).

Fig. 8

Begin by picking up a stitch in the first chain (*Fig. 9*) and in each chain around, skipping the last chain. Remember that the loop on the Knook counts as your first stitch.

Fig. 9

Before beginning your first round, place a marker on the Knook before the first stitch to mark the beginning of the round (*Fig. 10*).

Fig. 10

You can slide the cord out of the stitches as you work or after each round is complete.

ZEROS

To shorten the length of a complex pattern, zeros are sometimes used so that all sizes can be combined. For example, K 0{1} means that the second size would knit one stitch and the first size would do nothing.

JOINING NEW YARN

Finish one row and cut that yarn leaving a 6" (15 cm) end. Begin the next row with the new ball of yarn, leaving a 6" (15 cm) end to weave in later. When you are working in the round, leave a 6" (15 cm) end of the old yarn and begin knitting with the new ball of yarn, also leaving a 6" (15 cm) end. If you leave the yarn ends long enough, the stitches will not come undone and you don't need to tie a knot. If you wish, you may tie a temporary single knot that will be untied later and the ends woven into the fabric.

CHANGING COLORS

When changing colors, always pick up the new color yarn from **beneath** the dropped yarn and keep the color which has just been worked to the left (*Fig. 11*). This will avoid holes in the finished piece. Take extra care to keep your tension even.

Fig. 11

INCREASING EVENLY ACROSS A ROW OR ROUND

Add one to the number of increases required and divide that number into the number of stitches on the Knook. The result is the number of stitches to be worked between each increase. (If it's not a whole number, round down.)

INCREASES

KNIT INCREASE (uses one st)

Knit the next stitch (*Fig. 12a*), then knit into the **back** loop of the **same** st (*Fig. 12b*).

Fig. 12a

Fig. 12b

MAKE ONE (abbreviated M1)

With yarn in back, insert the Knook under the horizontal strand between the stitches from the **back** to the **front** (*Fig. 13a*), then knit into that strand (*Fig. 13b*).

Fig. 13a

Fig. 13b

MAKE ONE PURL *(abbreviated M1P)*

With yarn in front, insert the Knook under the horizontal strand between the stitches from the **front** to **back** *(Fig. 14a)*, then purl into that strand *(Fig. 14b)*.

Fig. 14a

Fig. 14b

YARN OVER *(abbreviated YO)*

A yarn over is simply placing the yarn over the Knook creating an extra stitch. Since the yarn over produces a hole in the knit fabric, it is used for a lacy effect. On the row following a yarn over, you must be careful to treat it as a stitch by knitting it as instructed.

Bring the yarn to the front **under** the Knook, then back **over** the top of the Knook so that it is now in position to knit the next stitch *(Fig. 15)*.

Fig. 15

DECREASES
KNIT 2 STITCHES TOGETHER
(abbreviated K2 tog)

Insert the Knook into the **front** of the second and then the first stitch on the cord as if to **knit** *(Fig. 16a)*, then **knit** them together as if they were one stitch *(Fig. 16b)*.

Fig. 16a

Fig. 16b

PURL 2 STITCHES TOGETHER
(abbreviated P2 tog)

Insert the Knook into the **front** of the first 2 stitches on the cord as if to **purl** *(Fig. 17)*, then **purl** them together as if they were one stitch.

Fig. 17

SLIP 1, KNIT 1, PASS SLIPPED STITCH OVER *(abbreviated slip 1, K1, PSSO)*

Slip one stitch as if to **knit** *(Fig. 18a)*. Knit the next stitch. Pull the stitch just made through the slipped stitch **(Fig. 18b)**.

Fig. 18a

Fig. 18b

KNIT 3 STITCHES TOGETHER
(abbreviated K3 tog)

Insert the Knook into the **front** of the third, the second, and then the first stitch on the cord as if to **knit** *(Fig. 19a)*, then **knit** them together as if they were one stitch *(Fig. 19b)*.

Fig. 19a

Fig. 19b

KNOOK BASICS

Using the Knook to create amazing knitted projects is fun and so easy! Let our step-by-step Basic Instructions show you how it's done. They're written and photographed for both left- and right-hand knooking. You'll get off to a fast start and be ready to create any of these beautiful hats. Be sure to visit LeisureArts.com to see the video versions of these instructions—every stitch and technique in this book is there, plus a few more! You'll also find free patterns for more Knook designs!

KNOOK PREP
Thread the cord through the hole at the end of the Knook. Gently pull the cord so that one end is approximately 8" (20.5 cm) from the Knook *(Fig. A)*, leaving a long end.

Fig. A

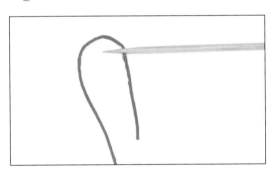

HOLDING THE KNOOK

There are two ways to hold the Knook. Hold the Knook as you would hold a pencil **(Fig. B)**, or as you would grasp a table knife **(Fig. C)**. Find the manner that is most comfortable for you.

Fig. B
Right-handed

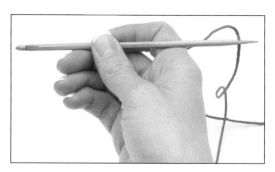

Left-handed

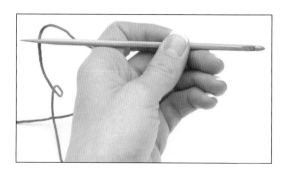

Fig. C
Right-handed

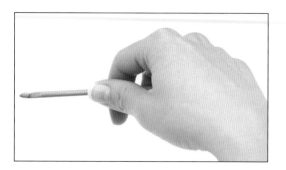

Left-handed

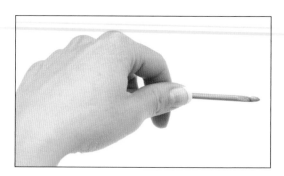

SLIP KNOT

The first step is to make a slip knot. Pull a length of yarn from the skein and make a circle approximately 8" (20.5 cm) from the end and place it on top of the yarn. The yarn on the skein-side of the circle is the working yarn, the opposite end is the yarn tail.

Slip the Knook under the yarn in the center of the circle *(Fig. D)*, then pull on both ends to tighten *(Fig. E)*.

Fig. D
Right-handed

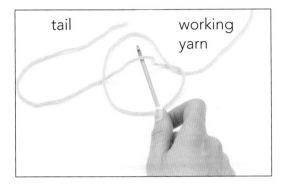

Left-handed

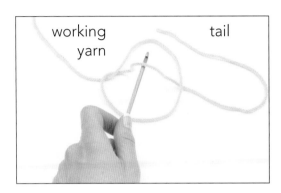

Fig. E
Right-handed

Left-handed

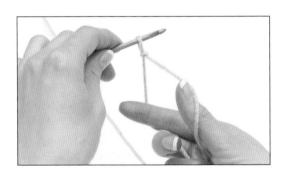

FOUNDATION CHAIN

Once the slip knot is on the Knook, the next step is to chain the required number of stitches, which is called the foundation chain.

With the Knook in your preferred hand, hold the slip knot with your thumb and middle finger of your other hand. Loop the working yarn over your index finger, grasping it in your palm to help control the tension of your yarn as you work the stitches *(Fig. F)*.

Fig. F
Right-handed

Left-handed

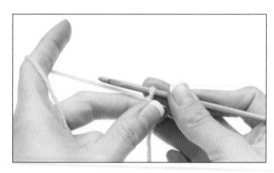
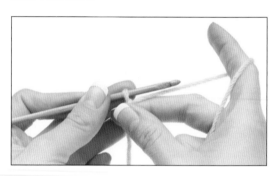

Wrap the yarn around the Knook from **back** to **front** *(Fig. G)*.

Fig. G
Right-handed

Left-handed

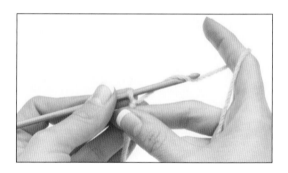

Turn the Knook to catch the yarn and draw the yarn through the slip knot *(Fig. H)*. Each time you wrap the yarn and draw the yarn through, you make one chain *(abbreviated ch)* of the foundation chain.

Fig. H
Right-handed

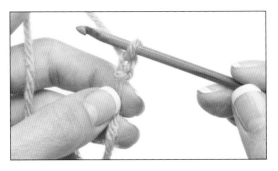

Left-handed

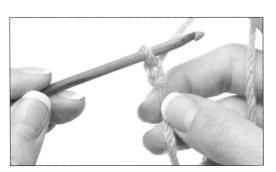

Repeat these steps to make the required number of chains.

If you already know how to crochet, please study the photos closely. From this point on, you will **NOT** be using the same yarn over typically used in crochet.

PICKING UP STITCHES

The loop on your Knook counts as the first stitch *(abbreviated st)*. To pick up the next stitch, insert the Knook from **front** to **back** into the second chain from the Knook *(Fig. I)*. With the Knook facing down, catch the yarn *(Fig. J)* and pull the yarn through the chain *(Fig. K, page 32)*.

Fig. I
Right-handed

Left-handed

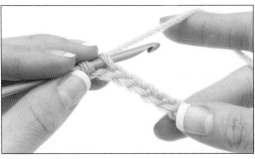

Fig. J
Right-handed

Left-handed

Fig. K
Right-handed   Left-handed

Repeat until you have picked up a stitch in each chain across *(Fig. L)*.

Fig. L
Right-handed   Left-handed

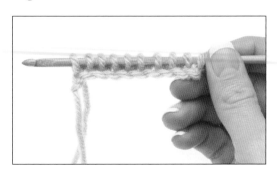
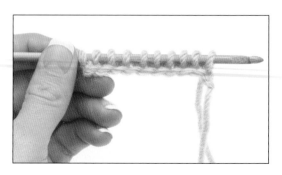

Slide the stitches off the Knook onto the cord *(Fig. M)*, allowing the short end to hang freely *(Fig. N)*.

Fig. M
Right-handed   Left-handed

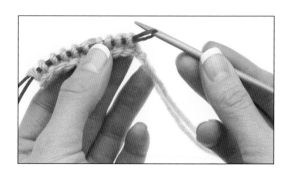

Right-handed

Left-handed

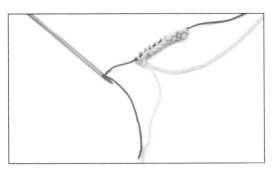

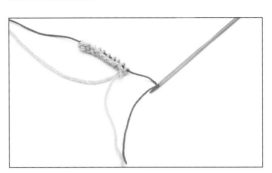

Turn your work around so that the working yarn and the yarn tail are closest to the Knook *(Fig. O)*.

Fig. O
Right-handed

Left-handed

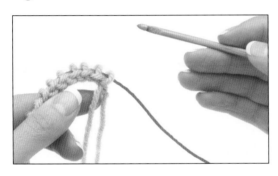

With the Knook in your preferred hand, hold your work with your other hand. Loop the working yarn over your index finger *(Fig. P)*.

Fig. P
Right-handed

Left-handed

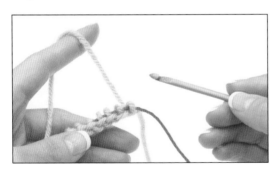

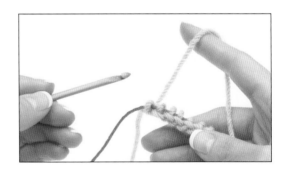

KNIT STITCH

Hold the work with the yarn to the **back**.

For right-handers, insert the Knook from **left** to **right** into the first stitch *(Fig. Q)*.

Fig. Q
Right-handed

For left-handers, insert the Knook from **right** to **left** into the first stitch *(Fig. Q)*.

Fig. Q
Left-handed

With the Knook facing down, catch the yarn *(Fig. R)* and pull it through the stitch, forming a knit stitch on the Knook *(Fig. S)*.

Fig. R
Right-handed

Left-handed

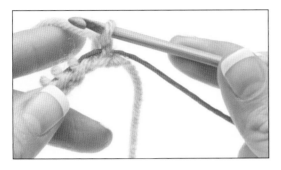
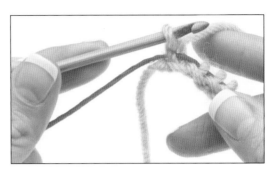

Keeping the yarn to the **back** of your work, repeat this process for each stitch across. Count the stitches to make sure you have the same number of stitches *(Fig. T)*.

Fig. T
Right-handed   Left-handed

If you do not have the required number of stitches, it is very easy to fix it at this point. Simply pull the Knook back out in the opposite direction you were working until you get to the mistake, and pull the yarn to undo the stitches.

Once each stitch has been worked, gently pull the long end of the cord out of the work, leaving the new stitches on the Knook *(Fig. U)*.

Fig. U
Right-handed   Left-handed

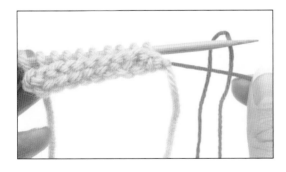
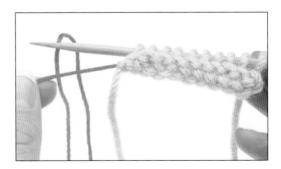

Slide the stitches off the Knook onto the long end of the cord, then turn the work.

PURL STITCH
Hold the work with the yarn to the **front**.

For right-handers, insert the Knook into the stitch from **right** to **left** (*Fig. V*).

Fig. V
Right-handed

For left-handers, insert the Knook into the stitch from **left** to **right** (*Fig. V*).

Fig. V
Left-handed

With the Knook facing away from you, wrap the yarn from **front** to **back** (*Fig. W*).

Fig. W
Right-handed

Left-handed

Catch the yarn with the Knook and pull the yarn through the stitch forming a purl stitch on the Knook (*Fig. X*). Keeping the yarn to the **front** of your work, repeat this process for each stitch across. Once each stitch has been worked, gently pull the long end of the cord out of the work, leaving the new stitches on the Knook.

Fig. X
Right-handed

Left-handed

Slide the stitches off the Knook onto the long end of the cord, then turn the work.

Working the knit stitch on every row creates a fabric called Garter Stitch. You will also create Garter Stitch if you purl every row.

Garter Stitch

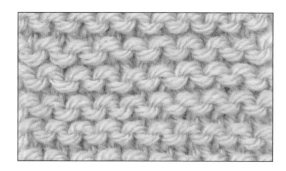

If you alternate knitting one row, then purling one row, the resulting knitted fabric is called Stockinette Stitch.

Stockinette Stitch
(right side)

Stockinette Stitch
(wrong side)

BIND OFF

Binding off is the method used to remove and secure your stitches from the Knook cord so that they won't unravel.

To bind off all the stitches in knit, knit the first two stitches. Pull the second stitch through the first stitch (*Fig. Y*).

Fig. Y
Right-handed

Left-handed

One stitch should remain on the Knook *(Fig. Z)*. Knit the next stitch and pull it through the stitch on the Knook.

Fig. Z
Right-handed   Left-handed

Repeat this process until there are no stitches on the cord and only one stitch remains on the Knook *(Fig. AA)*.

Fig. AA
Right-handed   Left-handed

Pull the cord out of the work. Cut the yarn, leaving a long end to weave in later. Slip the remaining stitch off the Knook, pull the end through the stitch, and tighten the stitch.

YARN INFORMATION

Each Hat in this leaflet was made using Medium Weight Yarn. Any brand of medium weight yarn may be used. It is best to refer to the yardage/meters when determining how many skeins to purchase. Remember, to arrive at the finished size, it is the GAUGE/TENSION that is important, not the brand of yarn. For your convenience, listed below are the yarns used to create our photography models.

2-STITCH CABLE PATTERN
Patons® Classic Wool
#77531 Currant

4-STITCH CABLE PATTERN
Patons® Classic Wool
#00231 Chestnut Brown

CHEVRON LACE PATTERN
Caron® Simply Soft®
#0014 Pagoda

CIRCLES HAT
Bernat® Satin
#04609 Goldenrod

EASY LACE PATTERN
Stitch Nation by Debbie Stoller™ Bamboo Ewe™
#5625 Sprout

SIDEWAYS GARTER STITCH HAT
Lion Brand® Vanna's Choice®
Magenta - #144 Magenta
Grey - #151 Charcoal Grey

TASSEL HAT
Red Heart® Soft Yarn®
#9939 Jeweltone

We have made every effort to ensure that these instructions are accurate and complete. We cannot, however, be responsible for human error, typographical mistakes, or variations in individual work.

Production Team: Writer/Technical Editor: Linda A. Daley; Editorial Writer - Susan McManus Johnson; Senior Graphic Artist - Lora Puls; Graphic Artist - Kara Darling; Photo Stylist - Angela Alexander; and Photographer - Jason Masters.